PLANET PATROL

A Kids' Action Guide to Earth Care

by MARYBETH LORBIECKI
illustrated by NANCY MEYERS

TWO CAN ™

MINNETONKA, MINNESOTA

CONTENTS

Attention, Earthlings!

As members of the Planet Patrol, it's our mission to join forces to protect the earth from overuse and abuse. Just like you, we love our planet—its blue skies and water, its green trees and colorful flowers, its amazing animals of all shapes, sizes, and incredible abilities, and all its different people. And believe it or not, we're all related. We're made of the same stuff: water, minerals, small living building blocks called cells, and some mysterious power called life.

The Planet Patrol always needs new members, and this book is your ticket! You'll find out how your planet works and how to do your part to help protect its environments. You will learn about the science of ecology, fun facts, new technologies, and action tips. So you can always leave your place on earth better than you found it.

In the first section, called Wildlife Watch, you'll meet some of the planet's amazing animals and plants. Section two, Eco Challenges, focuses on global issues such as air and water quality. And in Daily Defense, you'll learn about things you can do to make a difference at home and while shopping.

This is the only planet we've got, so we've got to get started now!

Dmitri Kare-Enoff   Esperanza La Paz

Dr. Mir Cosmos

CAPTAINS OF THE PLANET PATROL

The More Kinds, the Better

Have you ever taken apart a radio or computer and tried to put it back together? There are hundreds of pieces, and it's hard to tell what they all do. But if one part is missing, a job won't get done. Other parts won't be able to do their jobs either.

The earth works the same way. Different places, such as small areas of woods, ocean, desert, or rain forest, are called **habitats**. Each habitat has its own kind of soil, landscape, weather patterns, and mix of plants and animals. All these parts work together.

Scientists often judge how healthy a place is by how many different **species**, or kinds, of creatures and plants live in an area. For example, in a healthy stream you may find stone flies and dragonflies, skinks and frogs, snails, clams, and many kinds of fish. The more different species there are in one place, the more jobs get done, the more food is made and eaten, and the more healthy a place is. That's **diversity**.

The Forest Police

Red ants have the nickname "the Forest Police." They guard little green aphids from predators, because they like the sweet juice the aphids make from the sap of pine trees. The juicy droppings also attract bees. As the bees buzz about, looking for the tasty aphid juice, they spread pollen from tree to tree. Each bit of pollen helps make seeds that can sprout into new pine trees. To stay healthy and growing, the pine forest needs all three of these insect species, not just one!

How to Heal a Habitat

In Kenya, a cement company had stripped the top layers of soil and stone from 900 acres of land. This left a dusty, rocky place without trees, grass, or flowers. But a scientist named Dr. René Haller had a plan to heal this habitat. In the early 1970s, he dug into the crumbly limestone and planted hardy, fast-growing trees and grasses. After a layer of dead leaves piled up, he added millipedes. These bugs ate the leaves and left droppings that helped improve the soil. Then Dr. Haller made fishponds and brought in larger wild animals, such as antelope and oryx. The animals drank at the ponds and ate the leaves, bark, and grasses. The animals' manure made the soil richer, and more plant and animal species appeared. Then lions moved in to hunt. Because of Dr. Haller's efforts, local people can now fish and hunt here. Others have jobs working to restore the land. "It's surprising what nature can do when you lend a helping hand," said Dr. Haller.

"Good work, you guys!"

ACTION TIP – SPECIES COUNT

List all the species you can find in your backyard, schoolyard, or park. Sort the species into plants, insects, birds, reptiles, amphibians, fish, and mammals. You can look them up in field guides. See how many different species live right alongside you!

We Are All Related

Doctors study how a body works, and **ecologists** study how the earth and its habitats work. They want to discover the relationships between species, and how each species relates to the land, water, and air.

Like a spiderweb, everything in nature is connected in many different ways. Some species share homes. (I bet you have ants in your house!) Others eat the same food—or each other. Some animals live in the fur or hair of other animals or clean their hosts' teeth. All species depend on others for survival. Scientists call these webs of life **interdependency.** And if just one species in a web is removed, the whole web is harmed.

A Wasp Saves the Day

During the winter, the only trees in the Amazon rain forest that produce fruit are fig trees. Toucans, bats, monkeys, and many other animals live off the figs to keep from starving. Jaguars live off of these fig-eaters.

Even though the animals don't know it, they all

"I'll have what he's having."

Fig Wasps

depend on one little insect—a wasp! The small fig wasp burrows into the flowers of fig trees to lay its eggs. The flowers turn to fruit, and the eggs hatch. Then young males chew a tunnel out of the fruit. As the young females fly to new fig flowers to lay eggs, they carry pollen with them. Each fig tree must be visited by a fig wasp to make new seeds. If this species were to die out, so would the figs, and then the toucans, bats, monkeys, jaguars, and many other animals in the forest would have little to eat through the winter.

Otters and Urchins

Sea otters love to eat crabs. So do people. Crab fisherman used to kill otters so there would be more crabs for them to catch. But when the otters disappeared, so did the seals and bald eagles. Why? Because seals and eagles depend on otters. Besides crabs, otters also eat sea urchins, and the urchins eat sea plants. Without otters, the sea urchins multiplied. The urchins ate up most of the kelp and sea grasses in the area. The fish that lived among these sea plants swam away. The seals and eagles that ate the fish had to look for new homes, too.

Eventually, crab fishermen got the point. They stopped hunting otters, and the sea plants grew back. Soon the fish, seals, and eagles returned. Nature was back in balance.

ACTION TIP – BE A SPECIES SPY!

Pick a species that lives near you—it could be in a garden, pond, park, or yard. Visit the place it lives every day at the same time and watch the species quietly for 15 to 30 minutes. Keep a journal with notes and/or sketches. Does your species act differently when the weather changes or when other animals are near? Pretty soon you'll get to know that animal—how it acts and how it is connected to other species.

Saving Species

Did you know that pandas, snow leopards, mountain gorillas, Atlantic salmon, green sea turtles, and blue whales may soon become **extinct**? They could disappear from the earth forever. Right now, thousands of mammals, birds, insects, fish, reptiles, amphibians, and plants you've never even heard of are struggling to stay alive. Other species have already been wiped out.

Scientists and governments label struggling species as **endangered** (at serious risk of dying out) or **threatened** (almost endangered). The main reasons that species become endangered are:

- ☹ Loss of their habitat
- ☹ Invasion by a new species that takes away their homes or food, or brings deadly diseases
- ☹ Too much hunting, trapping, or poisoning
- ☹ Pollution
- ☹ Major changes in weather patterns

To learn more, read on, and don't stop till you get to the end of the book. Once you understand why a species is in danger, you can join others to protect it!

ENDANGERED.

green sea turtle

ENDANGERE

panda

Schoolyard Scientists

Why are burrowing owls becoming rarer? To find out, students in Fort Myers, Florida, built owl perches on their playground so they could watch the owls and take notes. Their observations became part of the University of Florida's study on burrowing owls and their habitat needs. Kids at other schools have joined in wildlife research projects. Fifth-graders in Baltimore used Eye of the Falcon software to track young bald eagles around Chesapeake Bay. Perhaps researchers at a university or nature center near you could use your help.

Burrowing Owl

ENDANGERED! snow leopard

ENDANGERED! mountain gorilla

How to Save a Mint

In California, school-children discovered that a rare desert plant called the San Diego mesa mint lived in only two places on the earth. One site was nearby—and a home builder was about to bulldoze it!

The school's ecology club alerted the state's Department of Fish and Game. They wrote letters to the local newspaper, made door-to-door visits, and held neighborhood meetings. They let everyone know what was happening, and they saved a mint!

A Howling Good Time

The woods of Wisconsin were once home to many wolves. But by 1960, every wolf in the state had been shot, poisoned, trapped, or driven into Canada. Without these **predators**, deer herds grew too large. The herds stripped forests of bark and leaves. By the end of each winter, many deer had starved.

To help the state bring back the wolves, children in northern Wisconsin joined the Adopt-a-Wolf program. They taught adults not to be afraid of wolves and helped pay for adding new wolves to the wild. Slowly, the wolves returned, and the forests and deer herds grew healthier.

"Scientists say over 12,000 animal and plant species may go extinct very soon."

ACTION TIP – NATURE'S CALL

Call a local nature center or your state's office of the U.S. Fish and Wildlife Service to find out about the endangered species near you. (You can also visit the website of the National Wildlife Federation.) Pick a species and research its habits and habitat. Find out what can be done, and start your own club to help save your species.

Home Sweet Habitat

A habitat is a species' home, but it's a community too! It's a place where species live together, naturally finding the things they need to survive—food, water, shelter, places to roam and to rest.

Hundreds of different species live in a habitat. Some beings are so tiny you can't see them without a microscope. Others are huge, like a moose or a whale. No matter how big or how small we are, everyone needs a habitat. That's why protecting habitats is as important as protecting species.

Double and Triple Trouble

Many of North America's prettiest summer species—our brightly colored songbirds and butterflies— are **migratory**. They spend their winters in rain forests

near the equator. Each spring, they fly thousands of miles to stay with us for the summer. If we want to keep seeing them, we've got to save rain forests down south as well as habitats here—and don't forget some rest-stops along the way!

Sand County Turnaround

In 1935, a naturalist named Aldo Leopold bought some land ruined by bad farming, leaving old cornfields with no topsoil, few trees, and piles of sand. The Leopold family went to work, planting thousands of trees and a meadow of prairie grasses and wildflowers. They used buckets to haul water to the new plantings. Within ten years, many different trees, grasses, and

flowers were growing on their own. The sandy wasteland had become a mixture of forest, prairie, marsh, and river, all alive with wildlife. Aldo Leopold wrote: "When we see land as a community to which we belong, we may begin to use it with love and respect."

Stop Those Invaders!

Gypsy Moth Caterpillar

Did you know plants and animals can become bullies? Species that have been moved from their natural habitats to new places are called **exotic species**. Since they have no natural enemies, their numbers grow too quickly. They push out **native species** (the ones that belong there) and eat their food. One example is

Starling

Eurasian milfoil, which came from tropical fish tanks. Some other invaders are killer bees, English house sparrows, fire ants, gypsy moths, and starlings.

Never add a species from one habitat to another, especially one from a faraway place.

Prevent Pet Bullies

Pets can be invaders too! Cats and dogs kill millions of songbirds and small wildlife each year. If only one pet cat in ten kills one bird a day, 4.4 million birds die. So put bells on your pets' collars and keep them from wandering.

ACTION TIP – MAP YOUR HABITAT

Draw a map of your habitat. Where is your home and where do you roam? How far does your food and water have to travel to get to your habitat? What other species share your habitat? What dangers are in your habitat?

City Welcome

Wherever you live, you can invite wild species to join you. If you live in a house, look no further than your yard. Plant a garden, prairie, or grove of trees. Add bird-houses and feeders, and leave a dead tree, a patch of sand, or a brush pile. If you live in an apartment, plant window boxes for butterflies or place potted trees on your balcony for the birds. Flat roofs are great for rooftop retreats!

Your school or city may also have a space that needs some habitat building. (Schools can even win money to do this.) You can connect with other schools doing habitat building through the Internet.

Just remember that animals need the same things people do: food, water, homes to have their babies, and places to run and hide.

Making a Splash of It!

Wild animals seek out water for drinking, bathing, or just playing around. Pick a spot 15 feet (5 m) from bushes, where cats can hide. Scoop a hole in the dirt, and lay an old garbage-can lid in it upside–down. Fill it with water. (Change the water every few days.) If it's under a tree branch or clothesline, hang a bucket of water with a few holes above it for a drip shower. Then watch to see who comes to sip and splash.

Less Lawn, More Habitat

Is your family tired of watering and mowing? Plant a lawn of native grass, such as buffalo grass. It will need less watering and mowing, and no chemicals. Some people with lawns and gardens put up to ten times more chemicals on one acre of soil than farmers do. And these chemicals kill some of the wildlife species in your yard. They're bad for people and pets, too. So plant native grasses and let nature keep your lawn lovely and full of wildlife.

Building from Rubble

In 1986, North Philadelphia had many trashy vacant lots. An artist named Lily Yeh encouraged neighborhood kids to pick up the junk in one of the lots. She showed them how to make mosaic tree sculptures using cement and bits of trash, such as bottle caps and glass shards. Then the group added benches and planted real trees. They turned the ugly lot into a colorful public park that attracts birds and people.

From this project, an organization called The Village of Arts and Humanities got its start. The group has now transformed more than 150 abandoned city lots into parks, vegetable gardens, green spaces, and a tree farm. They celebrate with planting activities, harvest festivals, art exhibits, and theater. The kids and their communities learn how they can make places for wildlife and people to live joyfully and colorfully together. The Village has even helped kids make new habitats out of ruined spots in Kenya, Ecuador, and other countries.

ACTION TIP – TOAD HAVEN

Want to welcome toads to your garden? Just overturn a broken cup or clay pot, and leave it in a cool, shady spot. For more ideas and directions in building habitats and attracting wildlife, go to your library or get involved in the National Wildlife Federation's Backyard and Schoolyard Habitat Programs.

Country Living

Farm families, with their large plots of land, play an important role in protecting wildlife and habitats. Some farm in a new way called **sustainable** farming. Sustainable farmers use natural products and methods that sustain the land, or keep it strong. Instead of using chemicals, they use **compost** and manure to fertilize their fields. They move their crops from year to year to give the soil a rest. They leave some trees, wild areas, brush piles, and dead trees to attract wildlife and hold down the **topsoil**. Animals are given plenty of room to graze so the grass they eat has a chance to grow back.

This kind of farming isn't easy, but it is rewarding and often less expensive than other ways of farming. It's working WITH nature, not against it!

The Soil's Alive!

Topsoil is the rich, dark top layer of dirt. It's made of dead stuff—plants, leaves, and animals—along with animal droppings. But it is also alive—with insects, earthworms, slugs, and tiny living things called **microorganisms.** These creatures slowly break down the dead things into little bits called **nutrients.** The plant roots absorb these nutrients as food.

It takes the earth a long time to make topsoil. Yet thousands of tons of topsoil are lost each year from unplanted farm fields and construction sites. Without topsoil, only a few tough plants can grow, and the land becomes desert-like. But you can help! Plant trees, bushes, and native grasses. The roots hold the topsoil so it won't be carried away by wind or rain.

Highway Havens

Did you know that the land along roads can be made into wildlife habitats? Kids and adults are setting up birdhouses and picking up litter. They're working with highway departments to plant native grasses and flowers and trees.

Dust Bowl

In the 1930s, no rain and poor farming created the "Dust Bowl" in America's

farmlands. The topsoil turned to dust and blew away. Some dirt from Kansas blew all the way to Washington, D.C.! To prevent a future disaster, farmers started planting trees around their fields to protect them from the wind.

Farm Assistants

Many farmers and gardeners use chemicals to stop mice, insects, and other pests from ruining their crops. But nature is less expensive! Hawks, bats, and ladybugs eat garden pests for free. Hummingbirds, butterflies, and bees carry pollen from plant to plant so new seeds can develop.

ACTION TIP – TAKE A LOOK!

Scoop up some soil. Spread it on a white paper plate. Pick out the rocks and sand. What do you have left? Make a list. Did you find leaves, sticks, seeds, bugs, or worms? Draw pictures of the live things you see. Use a magnifying glass or microscope to take an even closer look at your soil. What new things do you see?

Water Wonderlands

Wherever land meets water, incredible habitats are born. Birds, turtles, and amphibians nest in the sand. Fish feed and spawn in water near the shore. Insects skim, flitter, and fly.

Maybe you live near an ocean or lake, river or pond, wetland or tide pool, and have watched all this excitement. The best way to keep that wonderland healthy is to help people understand how to protect it: keep lawns, livestock, and construction sites away from the water. They all cause the soil to **erode**, or break down into little pieces that wash into the water. This dirt, called **sediment**, clogs the water and makes it harder for species to survive.

Chemicals are another serious problem for watery habitats. Whether the chemicals wash off of nearby lawns or get dumped into the water by storm sewers or factories, they poison the water.

Few things are uglier or smellier than a dead body of water, killed by pollution, litter, and too much sediment. That is why it's so important to protect our waters *and* their shorelines.

Restore a Shore— Buffer It!

To protect your water habitat, make a shore buffer zone. Plant bushes, trees, and tall grasses near the water. If you have a lawn, don't mow all the way down to the shore. If trees fall into the water, leave them alone—they make great nurseries for fish, frogs, birds, and other animals. Soon you'll find cleaner water and more wildlife.

Kids Join the Scientists

You don't have to be a scientist to take part in important water studies! Students at Coupeville Middle School, on an island in Puget Sound, Washington, joined with the Monterey Bay Aquarium to explore their waters. Sitwell School students adopted streams and shorelines around Chesapeake Bay, in Maryland. The Girls Club of Wilmington, Delaware, sent their scientific stone-fly counts and water tests to Save Our Streams, a river conservation group. Students in Clear Lake, Wisconsin, restored a wetland at their school. If these kids can get involved, so can you!

"Did you know 94% of all life in a lake is born, raised, and fed within 30 feet of the shore?"

What's in a Wetland?

Wetlands—marshes, swamps, and bogs—are some of nature's food factories. Algae, marsh reeds, and water lilies turn the sun's energy and muddy minerals into leaves and flowers. Moose and ducks feed off these plants. The wetlands' fish, water bugs, and flying insects become food for birds, larger fish, and reptiles. These species, in turn, are eaten by hawks, wolves, coyotes, and people.

But making food is only one of the wetland's jobs. It also works as nature's water-treatment plant. The plants' roots suck up minerals and water, along with chemicals and other poisons, leaving the water a little cleaner than it was before. Water also seeps into the layers of wetland mud. These layers trap more chemicals before the water sinks underground or flows into rivers and streams.

ACTION TIP – TAKE A WALK ON THE WILD SIDE

Stroll to a shore with a buffer zone. Count the species you see (especially insects). Scoop water into a cup. Smell it. Let the dirt settle. Does the water look clean? Then go to a shore with a lawn near the water to do the same things. Can you see any differences?

Go Wild!
Saving Parks & Wilderness

Can you imagine a place where you can't hear a lawnmower, car, truck, jet ski, or ATV? Where you can see the night stars clearly, without distracting lights?

Beautiful wild places like this exist in some of our large parks, refuges, and green spaces. In special areas called **wilderness**, motors are not allowed. Visiting these wild spots can be a taste of heaven. We can make campfires, gaze at the stars, smell the pines, and observe rare wildlife. We learn how to become part of nature without dirtying it up or making big changes. In addition, these wild places serve as scientific examples of how certain ecosystems and habitats work most naturally. They provide habitats for large predators, such as wolves, bears, and mountain lions, and species that are shy of humans.

The wilderness motto is "Enjoy and Leave No Trace." That means leave no sign you've been there—except the photos you bring back!

Envy of the World

Did you know the United States and Canada are planet leaders in preserving wild places? People from around the globe come to enjoy North America's parks and wildernesses. Then they return home excited to protect the few wild places they have left.

Good for the Spirit

Going into the wilderness gives us a chance to enjoy the beauty, calm, and adventure nature can give us. We move around by our own powers—hiking, canoeing,

backpacking, kayaking—or with the help of horses and burros. There are no phones, e-mails, schedules, or lots of "stuff," because we can't carry it all in. This can be refreshing to the spirit.

In fact, spending time in wild places is part of many religious traditions and holy writings. That's why religious groups are helping to save wilderness areas —and the planet!

A Wild Economy

The better a wild place is protected, the more healthy and beautiful it is, and the more people want to visit it. They bring money to communities around the wilderness or park, and that makes jobs. So protecting wild places can also protect the pocketbooks of the people who live near them.

Please Do Not Disturb!

Animals need a rest too. Some animals are endangered because they spend so much energy escaping people, pets, and cars that they get too tired to find enough food for themselves and their young. So wherever you go, do your best not to disturb the wildlife. They need all their energy to survive.

ACTION TIP – BECOME A NATURE DETECTIVE

Some people know how to find tracks, feathers, droppings, rubbings on bark, and other signs and use them to tell what wild animals have been doing. Plants also tell them stories, such as when and where a forest fire, drought, or other big weather event happened. To learn how you can be a nature detective, stop at your library for books on wildlife signs, tracking, and on specific animals. Visit nature centers or join a scouting or Campfire group.

Breathing Hard

Thinking about air can be a breath-taking experience. Feel it as you breathe. Does it flow easily, or make your chest tight? Sniff it. Can you smell cut grass and flowering trees or something not so nice?

Air is made mostly of two gases: oxygen and carbon dioxide. Animals (that includes us!) use the oxygen (O_2) and breathe out the carbon dioxide (CO_2). In contrast, plants take in CO_2 and give back O_2. Nature is in balance, right?

The trouble is, we humans also have vehicles and other machines that produce CO_2, so the plants can't keep up. Plus, there are other forms of air pollution. Anything that gives off smoke, fumes, and gas causes problems: cars, trucks, and motorboats; lawn mowers and leaf blowers; barbecue grills and fires; factories and power plants; fertilizers and crop dust.

In the 1970s, laws were passed to make North American air cleaner, and they worked. That's something to cheer about! But big challenges remain.

> "Motor vehicles are the single, biggest source of air pollution in the world."

Asthma Attacks!

Guess who gets hurt most by air pollution—kids! That's because their lungs are still developing. Many health professionals think more children are getting asthma (an illness causing coughing, wheezing, and difficulty breathing) because of indoor and outdoor air pollution. The EPA—the United States' Environmental Protection Agency—now has a kids' web site with an air quality index (AQI). Using colors, it shows daily how safe the air is in major cities. So check it out!

Unsafe Indoor Air

You may think pollution is all outside. But indoors, mold, dust, lead, radon gas, and chemicals in carpets and building materials can pollute the air, too. So if you're having trouble breathing at home or school, ask for an air test.

Don't Forget Noise & Light Pollution!

If they bother us, think how much they bother wildlife, who are more sensitive to these things!

ACTION TIP – AIR TEST

Spread petroleum jelly inside four wide-mouth glass jars. Place one jar in your home and place one in a safe place outside. Put another in your classroom and one in a safe place outside your school. Keep a chart. After one week, compare the jars. Which jar is darkest? Look around. What things nearby could be causing pollution? What solutions can you suggest?

Pollution can mix with rain to make acid rain. This toxic mixture burns holes in leaves, making plants and trees more open to disease. Acid rain also ruins lakes and harms the fish (and anyone who eats them!).

Warming Weather

When too much carbon dioxide (CO_2) gets into the air, it wraps around the earth like a heavy blanket, warming up the planet. This dangerous change is known as **global warming**. It is making icy places such as Greenland, the Arctic, and Antarctica melt around the edges. This cold meltwater raises sea levels, cools sea temperatures, drops salt levels, and shifts the currents. These changes can kill ocean life. Sea levels are now rising at three times their usual rate. Eventually, the seas will begin to flood low, coastal areas, such as Venice, Italy, and much of Florida.

Global warming is also changing weather patterns, spreading hot-weather diseases to new areas, and changing plant and animal life in many ways. No one really knows what chain reactions these changes will cause in our lifetimes. Or our children's lifetimes. But the planets' most respected scientists are worried. While scientists and world leaders are talking and acting, so can we!

Nature Knows

Some people say that global warming isn't happening, and that weather is always changing. But scientists studying wild plants and animals are seeing patterns in the changes. Migrating birds are consistently coming to Wisconsin at least 10 days earlier in the spring and leaving 10 days later in the fall than they did in the 1930s. Flowers are blooming 10 days earlier, and growing seasons are ending 10 days later. In many places, the summer seasons are getting longer and hotter, and winters in northern and southern regions have less snow and ice.

Catching CO2

A new machine can suck some carbon dioxide out of the air and pump it into deep holes in the earth. But CO_2 can only be buried in very hard rock, because it mixes with water and makes an acid that eats away soft rock. This tricky but promising new technology may prove helpful in getting rid of a little of the CO_2 already out there.

A Hole in the Sky

Our planet has a protective shade around it called the **ozone layer**, which shields us from the sun's burning rays. However, the ozone layer is being thinned out by certain chemicals, such as chlorofluorocarbons, or CFCs. CFCs are used in aerosol spray cans, cleaners, foam, refrigerators, and freezers. In one area over the South Pole (near New Zealand and Australia), the ozone layer has developed an open hole. So wear sunscreen and sunglasses, and buy hair spray, paint, and cleaners in pump spray bottles or cans instead of aerosols. And write your government officials, asking them to stop companies from using dangerous ozone-thinning chemicals.

ACTION TIP – LOW-CAR DIET PLAN

For each mile you ride in a car (even a small car), one pound of CO_2 is put into the air. For a day, jot down every mile you ride in a car. Add these miles up. How many pounds did you put into the air in one day? Try it for a week. Can you think of ways to reduce these pounds for the next week?

☺ 40% of the world's oxygen comes from the Amazon rain forest.

☺ Many cancer-fighting drugs come from rain-forest plants. One of these, the rosy periwinkle, grows in only one place—the rain forest of Madagascar.

☺ Many things can be harvested from rain forests without cutting them down, including fruits such as bananas and oranges; spices such as cinnamon, paprika, and cloves; shade-grown coffee; rubber; nuts; cocoa beans; and wood oils.

Shrinking Forests

One cure for too much CO_2 is more trees. For every pound of new tree wood grown, two pounds of CO_2 are absorbed from the air. Unfortunately, around the world, forests are being cut far faster than they can grow back or be replanted. Some are being cleared permanently to make farm fields or cattle ranges. This is harming not just the places where the trees are cut, but the whole planet!

And trees are good for more than just cleaning the air. They give shade, so each tree makes a place cleaner and cooler. Their branches break the wind, stopping topsoil from blowing away. Their roots hold the soil in place. Animals use them for food and shelter. Can you think of anything more useful than a tree?

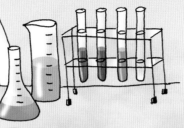

"Maybe the cure for cancer can be found in one of our rain forests."

☺ North America has rain forests, too. They are found in the Pacific Northwest: Oregon, Washington, and British Columbia. The bark of the yew trees there are used for cancer medicines.

Species Storehouses

Did you know that more species of ants live in one tree in a Peruvian rain forest than in all of England? Certain habitats, like rain forests and old-growth forests (wetlands and coral reefs too!) are jammed with species. This diversity makes them super important, for they are the earth's living storehouses.

Beat the Stock Market— Plant a Tree!

In the early 1990s, you could buy a tree seedling for $5. A scientist estimated that in 50 years, that tree would provide goods and services worth about $191,000: $31,000 for making oxygen; $61,000 for cleaning the air of dusts, CO_2, and other gases; $37,000 for absorbing water and breathing the moisture into the air for rain clouds; $31,000 for adding nutrients to the soil; and $31,000 for providing wildlife homes and food. In 50 years, it would be worth 38,200 times its original $5 price tag. This doesn't even count the benefits that are harder to measure: it increased the value of the land, cut noise levels, shaded and cooled nearby homes (without air conditioning!), held the soil in place, and made its surroundings more beautiful.

Wow, money really does grow on trees!

ACTION TIP – HOW MANY TREES DO YOU OWE?

It's estimated that by the time we reach 80 years old, we each owe the earth 2,000 trees—to balance out the CO_2 we've breathed out plus the CO_2 we've added through the use of cars and electricity from power plants. This total doesn't even count the trees we use up in wood and paper products. If you start this year, how many trees do you need to plant each year to reach 2,000 by the time you are 80 years old? Better join with friends and family and start planting!

Stumped?

If trees are worth so much alive, should we stop cutting them completely? No! Then we couldn't ever build things of wood. But some ways of cutting trees are better than others.

Clear cutting, or cutting all the trees in a large area at once, can be disastrous. It leaves the ground bare, so that wind and rain can tear the topsoil away. Nearby rivers and lakes become sludged with it. Shade plants and important soil organisms die.

Selective cutting is healthier. Loggers carefully cut some trees and leave the rest to grow. The remaining trees hold down the topsoil and make seeds. Then it's easier for the forest to grow back naturally. There are healthier ways to replant trees too. Scattering a mix of different ages and kinds of native trees is better than planting only one kind of tree in rows. Selective cutting and mixed plantings cost more money at first. But they also create more jobs and save the diverse life of our forests.

Still stumped? Here's the deal: We can harvest lumber, but we need to cut less and preserve more—especially in rain forests. And when we do cut, we need to use practices that help the forest grow back as naturally as possible.

Tree Treasures

Tree products are almost endless. Besides things like fruits, nuts, and sap, trees give us lumber and furniture, paints and glues, fabrics and carpets, paper and some plastics…even Ping-Pong balls and insulation! Thankfully, some of these products can now be made out of other materials to save trees.

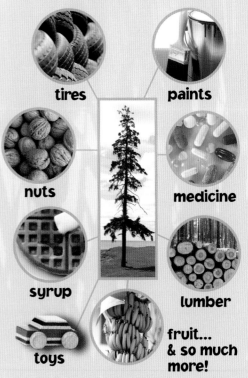

tires

paints

nuts

medicine

syrup

lumber

toys

fruit... & so much more!

Falling Giants

Some of the largest and oldest living things on earth live right here in North America. California's giant redwood trees grow taller than the Statue of Liberty, weigh as much as 800 school buses, and live to be 3,500 years old. Yet it takes just two hours to cut down one of these giants.

Planters for the Planet

After a forest fire in Indonesia, local Scouts planted 240 acres of trees. In Kenya, women's groups, schoolchildren, and communities have planted over 25 million trees. In El Segundo, California, third graders started the Tree Musketeers Club. (Kids in the club help other kids plant trees.) They also started an educational TV show, a water conservation program, and the Partners for the Planet Youth Summit. Think what you and your friends can do!

Partners for the Planet

"I made this paper from a pair of old blue jeans."

Paper Possibilities

To save trees, paper can be made out of other materials, such as old clothes, algae, sugarcane, drug-free hemp, and kenaf (a fast-growing, woody-stemmed plant).

ACTION TIP – ADDRESSING THE PAPER PROBLEM

In North America, most of the trees we cut are used to make paper. And over half the garbage we throw out is paper. That means we are turning our trees into trash! So what can we do? Cut down on paper use! And RECYCLE. Every time we recycle a ton of paper, we save 17 trees, conserve energy, and prevent pollution.

Sea Sickness

Oceans cover over three-fourths of the planet. Like forests, they give off moisture and oxygen and provide habitats for thousands of animals and plants. Unfortunately our oceans and marine wildlife are facing large troubles. Humans are polluting, poisoning, and changing the oceans in many ways:

- ☹ Oil spills from drilling and ships
- ☹ Soil, fertilizers, pesticides, and mining wastes that wash into the water
- ☹ Mercury and **acid rain** from polluted air
- ☹ Chemicals, sewage, and garbage dumped from ships and factories
- ☹ **Invasive species** carried in and on ships

Commercial fishing is adding to the problem. **Populations** of some fish, turtles, and other ocean animals are being harmed. Other animals are caught accidentally and die before they are thrown back. Still others get tangled in nets or lines and drown.

How can you help? Get to know your oceans and the amazing life in them. The more you know, the more you will be able to help protect them.

Where Has All the Color Gone?

Coral reefs and kelp beds are the ocean's rain forests. Coral reefs may contain over one-fourth of the ocean's species and may live to be 2.5 million years old. (They grow slowly!) But now these brightly colored reefs are turning white and dying. Pollution and temperature changes are weakening them. So some scientists are helping them by zapping the live coral with electricity. This improves their ability to use calcium from the water to build their reefs. But more than anything, the coral need protection from pollution.

Too Much Noise!

Sonar (sound-based radar) and ship and motor noises are confusing to sea animals. Dolphins use their own sonar to sense where objects are. Humpback whales sing melodies and listen carefully for answering songs. If we want these animals to find their way and communicate with other animals, we're going to have to cut the noise.

Kids to the Rescue!

In 1989, a group of kids in Alaska helped clean up after the tanker Exxon Valdez leaked oil. Sixth- and seventh-graders mucked around to count the injured and dead animals and plants. Their data has helped scientists understand oil spill effects. In 2002, Canadian high schoolers at a British Columbia leadership camp unveiled a technology they'd invented for faster oil-spill cleanup. To learn more about oil-spill cleanup efforts, visit the website of the Australian Maritime Safety Authority and play the "Fix-a-Slick" game.

Ocean Wilderness

Just as we need wild places on land, we need some under the sea and near it as well. It's time to set aside more underwater and shoreline spaces as motor- and fishing-free zones to give species safe places to have their young.

"Some of the most beautiful and amazing animals on earth live under the sea."

ACTION TIP – VISIT AN AQUARIUM

Take the time to read books about ocean life and visit aquariums. Beware of buying real seashells or sea animals such as sea horses or starfish. The people who sell these items often collect them while the animals are still alive. And if you find shells on the beach, be sure they are not occupied before bringing them home.

Wasting Away

Doesn't it seem like almost everything we do makes garbage? Food scraps, cans, bottles, packages, and wrappings are left after we eat. Paper and used envelopes pile up after we get the mail or do homework. There are broken games and toys, clothes we've outgrown, and books we no longer read. North Americans each throw away between 1,300 and 1,600 pounds (600–725 kg) of solid waste a year. How much do you weigh? Can you figure out how many times your own weight you create in garbage each year?

From sea to shining sea—and even under the sea—this garbage is piling up. Trash is dumped into landfills, down drains, into the ocean, into compost bins, and tossed around as litter. Some of these choices are better than others. But if we want to keep our planet from turning into one big garbage heap, we need to start rethinking what we buy and what we throw away.

Space Mess

Can you believe that there's even trash in space? Parts of spacecrafts, chips of paint, even tools have been left behind on the moon. Scientists think there are over 30,000 bits of garbage orbiting the earth. If a speeding spaceship hits just one floating sliver of trash, the ship will be damaged. So trash is dangerous, even in space!

"We've got a lot of cleaning up to do!"

United States 4 1/2 pounds
Canada 4 pounds
Sweden 2 pounds
Japan 1 3/4 pounds
Philippines 1 pound
Egypt 3/4 pound
Sri Lanka 3/4 pound
Ghana 1/2 pound

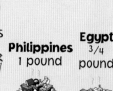

Trash around the World

Americans win first prize...for the amount of garbage they produce! The trash cans above show how much garbage the average person makes in different countries. People in poorer countries usually make less garbage than people in richer countries, because they buy fewer things and reuse more of them. Also, some countries encourage more reuse and less packaging.

Garbage Archeology

What will archeologists dig up centuries from now to learn about us? Probably trash in our landfills! There, garbage gets smashed so tightly that even things that are **biodegradable**, or able to rot and break down, don't have enough oxygen to do so. Sometimes poisonous gases develop. Here's how long some pieces of trash take to biodegrade even if they do have oxygen:

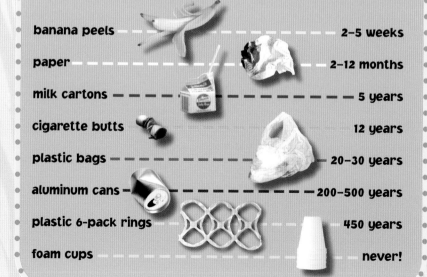

banana peels	2–5 weeks
paper	2–12 months
milk cartons	5 years
cigarette butts	12 years
plastic bags	20–30 years
aluminum cans	200–500 years
plastic 6-pack rings	450 years
foam cups	never!

ACTION TIP – DOWN WITH TRASH CONTEST

For one weekend, put all your personal trash in your own bag or basket. (Weigh the bag or wastebasket first.) At the end of the weekend, weigh the filled container. Subtract the weight of the bag or basket to find your total. How much trash did you make? How did your friends compare? The person who made the least trash wins. Share strategies for keeping trash totals down.

Garbage, the Great Resource

Did you know that much of the garbage we throw away can be reused? Some leftover food and lawn waste can be turned into **compost** for the soil. You can clean and pass on old clothes, or turn them into scarves, rugs, or rags. Empty bottles and jars can be cleaned and refilled. Worn tires can be made into shoes or purses, or ground into roadway material. Decorate a cake, gift bow, or mosaic with old toy figures. Plastic containers can be used for planting or for sorting and storing things.

If an item can't be fixed or reused, it can probably be **recycled** or transformed into a brand new object. Factories melt glass bottles and jars into new glass containers, marbles, decorative tiles, and even surfboards! Metal objects are melted down and molded into car and bike parts, cookware, and yes, new cans! Plastic bottles go into everything from park benches and playground equipment to ski jackets. Used paper and cardboard can be remixed into new paper and cardboard. As you can see, garbage is a great resource!

Trash to Cash

To earn money, kids around North America collect bottles, cans, ink cartridges, and cell phones. They sell these items to recycling companies. This helps the environment AND makes money for the kids' groups and schools. Everybody wins!

Borrow It!

You don't always have to buy something new. Try borrowing what you need instead. Just remember the borrower's motto: Always return something in better shape than you received it!

"Americans recycle more than half of all their aluminum beverage cans and large appliances."

Trashy Trivia

☺ North Americans are now recycling 28% of all their garbage. That is almost double what they did in 1993. But countries such as Austria, Belgium, Switzerland, and the Netherlands recycle at a rate of 70%.

☺ The United States recycles 42% of all paper and 40% of all plastic soft drink bottles. Even athletic shoes are being recycled!

☺ Some computer manufacturers take back used equipment and recycle the parts. Businesses and homeowners can donate their older computers to schools and nonprofit organizations.

☺ Recycling is good for the economy—it saves energy and materials PLUS creates jobs. The recycling industry employs more people than the mining industry and about the same number as the auto industry.

ACTION TIP – MAKE A SOIL FACTORY

Landfills get filled quickly with fall leaves, grass clippings, and food scraps. Why not turn this waste into soil? All you need is space for a pile or bin behind your home or school. Try this experiment to see how composting works. Take an old plastic container and fill it with veggie scraps, dry leaves, and grass clippings. Punch holes in the container and put it outside in the sun. Stir it up every few days. To speed up the process, add some worms! You can even ask your school to start a worm composting program to clean up school lunch scraps.

DAILY DEFENSE

Smart Shopping

The best way to cut down on garbage and pollution is to be careful what you buy. Here are some tips: First, buy only the things you need or really want. You will save yourself money and save the planet from too much stuff.

Second, choose items that are made to last. Save money and packaging by buying next-to-new items. When you're done with something that is still usable, bring it to a homeless shelter, the Salvation Army or Goodwill, a garage sale, or a second-hand shop.

Third, consider the packaging. Every month, Americans throw away their weight in packaging! Choose products that come in refillable or reusable containers. Some stores sell milk or soda in bottles that can be returned for cash. Next best are products in recyclable containers, such as glass bottles, recyclable plastics, and cans.

Finally, look for the products that are made in a safe and earth-friendly way, using recycled materials, nontoxic (not poisonous) and animal-friendly ingredients, and cruelty-free testing.

Do You Need It or Want It?

Commercials and ads are designed to make you think a product will make you better looking, more respected, happier, and healthier. But don't let yourself get tricked! Ask yourself: Do I need it? Or do I want it? Then decide if it's good for the planet and whether it's worth your money (and storage space).

When Is a Bargain Not a Bargain?

When something bought cheap breaks right away! If you have to buy the same item two or three times, it's NOT a bargain. It's expensive—and annoying.

Go Healthy, Go Organic

The food that's healthiest for you is the same food that's healthiest for the planet—organic! *Organic* means grown without chemicals or hormones.

The most fun kind of organic food is the kind you grow yourself. If you don't have a yard, see if your community rents out garden plots. You can also find organic foods at farmers' markets. These markets support local growers and use less packaging.

"Secondhand shops are a great place to find cool clothes!"

Meaty Matters

Eating meat is not always good for you, or for the planet. Around the world, thousands of acres of forest (especially rain forest) are cut down each year for grazing cattle. Many other animals, such as chickens, turkeys, and pigs, are kept in small, unhealthy cages or pens where they are fed chemicals and hormones to keep them from getting sick and to make them grow faster. We eat these substances when we eat the meat. To find the healthiest meat, look for packages marked "organic" and "free-range." These animals were fed natural foods and were given room to roam.

2 HDPE

OZONE FRIENDLY

CONTAINS **NO** CHLOROFLUORO CARBON PROPELLANT ALLEGED TO DAMAGE THE **OZONE** LAYER

ACTION TIP – SHOPPERS' BINGO

To help your family and friends become more aware, make some bingo cards with different combinations of planet-friendly symbols and terms: refillable, return for deposit, biodegradable, organic, free-range, cruelty-free, animal friendly, made of recycled materials, recyclable, chlorine free, non-aerosol (a planet-friendly spray can), dolphin-safe, low phosphorous or phosphorous-free, locally grown, grown without hormones, planet-friendly, and all-natural. You can probably think of more! Then go shopping and see who can fill up their bingo card first!

Transforming Transportation

It's a good thing our planet has as much creative energy as it has CO_2. Inventors and scientists are working hard to develop new fuels so that we can reduce the number of vehicles that use gasoline. Some of these new fuels are alcohols (methanol and ethanol), hydrogen gas, natural gas, liquid natural gas, battery-stored electricity, liquids made from coal, and **biodiesel fuels** made from plant oils or animal fat. Some cars can even run on sunshine! Their special engines are **solar powered**, soaking up energy from the sun's heat and using that to run their engines. They don't pollute at all.

Unfortunately, most of these new cars are still very expensive and hard to find. In the meantime, we need to change our habits more than our cars. So walk, skateboard, bike, or skate to get where you need to go. Share rides and do all your errands in one big trip. Take buses, subways, and trains.

Catch a Ride on the Future

All-electric or hybrid vehicles—those that run on a combination of electricity and gas—are showing up all over. These vehicles include cars, buses, trolleys, and light-rail trains. Some of the new trains are powered by magnets, while electric buses have special rechargeable batteries. Over thirty U.S. cities, such as New York City; Santa Clara, California; Anderson, Indiana; Cedar Rapids, Iowa; and Honolulu, Hawaii are running electric or hybrid buses. Universities and school districts are changing over too.

> **"The average piece of food eaten in America has traveled 1,300 miles. That's a lot of gas for one tomato!"**

Take the Veggie Van!

When you're in Yellowstone National Park, you may smell French fries when a bus goes by. That's because some Yellowstone buses run with on 20% recycled cooking oil (such as mustard seed or soybean oil) and 80% regular diesel fuel. Other Yellowstone buses run on pure biodiesel fuels. These fuels, made from animal or veggie fats, are biodegradable, or able to rot away, and the exhaust is not harmful. There are already some vehicles that run on old cooking grease. Perhaps someday you will pull up your car to a fast-food restaurant and say, "Fill 'er up!"

Race for Clear Skies

Every spring, student teams and car manufacturers enter their new, earth-friendly vehicles in the Swiss Tour de Sol or the American Tour de Sol. Cars are judged on how easy they are on the environment and how well they perform.

Some cars reach 127 miles per gallon (54 km per liter) with 1/7 of the exhaust of a regular car. The U.S. Department of Energy sponsors the Junior Solar Sprint for solar-powered cars created by sixth-, seventh-, and eighth-grade students. So start inventing!

ACTION TIP – MAP YOUR WAY TO CLEANER AIR

Find or make a map of your neighborhood. Mark the locations of your school, your friends' homes, parks, gyms, place of worship, places you shop or hang out. Now map the safest routes for biking or walking to these places. If there aren't sidewalks, bike paths, or bike lanes, talk to your neighborhood group or the city or town council.

Water Wisdom

What is more precious than gold or silver? Water! No one can live without it, and there is only so much clean fresh water on the planet. Wars are even fought over control of water sources. Yet, every day, we waste it.

How much water does your family use in a day? Consider this: It takes 5 to 7 gallons (19–26 l.) to flush an average toilet, 35 to 60 gallons (132–227 l.) to take a shower, and 10 gallons (45 l.) to wash a sink full of dishes. And many people spend gallons and gallons of water on their lawns. (Have you ever noticed sprinklers on even when it's raining?) Then consider the cleaners and chemicals we wash down our drains and toilets. Many of these are dangerous for both humans and wildlife.

That's why we need to think much more about how we treat the water we have. Remember, every drain washes into a body of water—a lake, river, wetland, ocean, or underground pool. All of these bodies of water are habitats for other animals.

You, too, probably live downstream of someone. So it's a good idea to do unto others what you want done unto you.

Drippy Facts

☹ If you leave the water running while you brush your teeth, you can waste 5 gallons (19 l.) of clean water. If you brush your teeth twice a day, that amounts to 3,650 gallons (13,817 l.) a year. That's enough to fill up a bathtub 150 times!

☹ A dripping faucet wastes 300 to 4,000 gallons (1,136–15,142 l.) of water per month.

38

"Yuck! Poor birds."

A Sticky Situation

A pint of motor oil that washes into water spreads out on the surface to make a one-acre oil spill. Hazardous, or dangerous, liquids such as paint, antifreeze, pesticides, pool chemicals, and mercury should NEVER be poured down drains, into storm sewers, or onto the soil. These should all be taken to drop-off centers.

Cleaning Up Cleaners

Household bleaches and cleaners are very poisonous—even the smell of them can make you sick. Think what it does to wildlife when they drink these liquids in their water! Using natural cleaners, such as vinegar or baking soda, with some elbow grease (hard scrubbing), is a lot better for everyone on the planet.

Water Alerts

Just because water comes from a faucet doesn't mean it's safe to drink. It could have lead or other chemicals in it. So if your water smells or tastes bad, don't drink it. Use a water filter first. Some filters fit on faucets. Another kind fits inside a pitcher. Pour your tap water into this pitcher, and put it into the refrigerator. You'll always have tasty, cold drinking water on hand. Don't forget to use filtered water for making ice cubes and for brushing your teeth!

ACTION TIP – WATER MAPPING

Call your local water department and ask where your drinking water comes from and where it flows once it goes down the drain. Make a water flowage map. Where does the water that drains from your home end up? Who lives upstream and downstream from you? What kind of wildlife?

Powerful Choices

What makes your lights go on, your computer work, and your TV run? Electricity. But what makes electricity? Most electricity is made in only a few ways—by burning coal, oil, gas, or garbage; through nuclear processes; or by capturing the power of river water with a dam.

All of these processes can be harmful. Burning materials puts smoke into the air. Coal mining usually strips the land of trees and topsoil, and leaves behind wastes that wash into rivers, lakes, and oceans. Drilling and shipping oil can lead to large oil spills. Nuclear energy doesn't give off air pollution, but it leaves behind extremely dangerous wastes that last for hundreds of thousands of years. Dams cause the fewest problems, because they are naturally powered by the water, but they change a river's habitat, which hurts fish and other wildlife. So what can we do?

We can make electricity with other natural energies, such as wind power, solar energy, ocean waves and tides, and geothermal heaters (powered by the earth's heat). These are all **renewable energies**, methods that take advantage of the earth's own powers. Scientists and inventors keep coming up with new and more efficient ways to tap these renewable sources. But until our power companies are using them, we need to try to conserve electricity, or use it more wisely—and waste less!

Pleasant Valley Is Pleasanter

This New York town provides power for its 10,000 citizens with wind power. Its changeover from a coal-burning power plant has saved the town from putting 356,000 pounds of CO_2 per year into the skies. The governor has pledged to make the wind the source of one-fourth of the state's power by 2013.

Coal Countdown

How much CO_2 is given off at a coal-burning plant to power your appliances?

Television	1 hour	.64 pounds
100-watt light bulb	10 hours	1.3 pounds
Clothes dryer	1 load	10 pounds
Refrigerator	1 day	12.8 pounds

That's why turning off anything you're not using is SO important!

"The average American uses enough energy a year to put 20.5 tons of carbon dioxide into the air."

Garbage Power

Garbage may soon provide electricity in a whole new way, with an invention called the Plasma Converter. It uses a stream of heat three times hotter than the sun to vaporize garbage.

Vaporizing the garbage breaks it down into its atomic elements, or its smallest mineral ingredients. The process not only gets rid of the garbage but produces clean-burning gases that can be used to create electricity.

ACTION TIPS: CONSERVING EVERY DAY

☺ Turn off the lights, radio, TV, CD or DVD player, and computer when you leave a room.

☺ During the winter, open your shades to let the sun in. Wear the "layered" look—a sweater or sweatshirt worn over another shirt—and turn down your furnace to 65 to 68 degrees Fahrenheit (18 to 20° C). Before snuggling into bed, turn it lower.

☺ During the summer, shut shades during the day to keep out the sun's heat. At night, open your windows to let in evening breezes. Save air conditioning only for the hottest of days!

☺ Wash dishes by hand, or, when using the dishwasher, fill it up completely, then stop it before the drying cycle. Let the air dry your dishes instead.

☺ Ask your parents to use energy-efficient light bulbs and appliances.

People Make a Difference

As you have seen, our actions really do add up. We all breathe, eat, go to school or work, and live someplace. These are natural things, because we are part of nature. Still, we have choices about HOW we do these things—in wise, responsible ways, or in careless ways that do more harm than good.

As the earth's population grows, sharing resources with each other and protecting wildlife becomes more of a challenge. In 2004, the world population reached 6.4 billion, and it is growing by 80 million people per year. Each day, 220,000 more people are born than have died.

Children are a natural and wonderful gift, and parents want to decide how big their family will be. Yet the world has limited land and fresh water, so it's important that we all think ahead and are careful about what we have.

Too Many People or Too Much Waste?

Q. Which is harder on the planet— 100 people, or 1 person who uses as much food, water, energy, and land as the 100 people and makes as much waste?

A. Neither. In richer countries, such as the United States, people use an average of 200 times more energy, water, and land than people in poorer counties. So even if families in less developed countries are larger, they use far fewer resources and have less of a harmful impact on the environment.

What's in a War?

When weapons are made, tested, and used, they cause deadly problems for the planet and for all of us.

☹ In recent wars, armies have set oil wells afire, caused oil and chemical spills, drained wetlands, polluted water, bombed or burned habitats, released disease-causing germs, and left behind dangerous weapons. This spoils the land and water for ages.

☹ Nuclear bomb testing leaves the area around a test site unhealthy for generations. These bombs can destroy life on the planet.

☹ Land mines don't stop working when a war ends. People are still being injured or killed by mines in Vietnam and Cambodia from wars in the 1970s.

☹ Ammunition made of depleted uranium gives off small doses of radiation (what a nuclear bomb gives off). In the first Gulf War in Iraq, 1,100 to 2,200 tons (1,000–2,000 t) of this ammunition was used in just two months. Since the war, Iraq has seen more birth defects in babies. This ammunition may be partly to blame for a sickness among American soldiers called Gulf War Syndrome.

ACTION TIP: BECOME A PEACEMAKER NOW!

Solving disagreements is a skill that needs to be learned and practiced. When you have a conflict with someone (or several people), try sitting at a Peace Table. Invite an uninvolved person to join you and keep the peace. Then take turns telling the different sides of the story respectfully. LISTEN WELL and find out what you can agree on. Never call people names, accuse them, or assume you know their reasons. Find a solution you can all live with. Knowing how to resolve a conflict peacefully is a skill you'll use your whole life!

Kid Power for the Planet

Kids in St. Lucia worked on a pipeline that brings clean water to island villages.

Kids in Thaila[nd] planted acr[es] of papaya tre[es]

When kids pay attention and care for the environment, they inspire adults to do it! That's why you have so much power.

You have seen stories of kids who have worked together with their parents, teachers, or group leaders to make their place on the planet cleaner or better for wildlife. There are so many more, they can't fit in this book! Kids in the U.S. have saved acres of woodlands and rain forests, and they have convinced McDonald's to use more earth-friendly packaging. Canadian kids have transformed yards and vacant lots into wildlife habitats. But the good work doesn't stop there. Around the world, the list of children's accomplishments is as endless as their imagination and commitment.

We know YOU too can help make the world a better place. Think about your favorite Planet Patrol ideas and get started. **The Planet Needs You!**

In Kenya, children taught conservation classes for adults.

Kids in the U.S. shared blankets with homeless people.

Egyptian kids cleaned up streets and parks.

Earth Day Is Every Day

RESPECT THE EARTH

In North America, people celebrate our planet on Earth Day, April 22. That leaves the rest of the year to do the work of taking care of it well!

ACTION TIP: PUTTING PAPER TO GOOD USE

To let local or national leaders know about a planet patrol problem, find out all the information you can on the subject from many sides first. (Don't forget the scientific information—you  can even call experts at universities.) Then you're ready to write. Begin with a few sentences that ask your questions or state your concerns. Then explain your ideas for a solution. Finally, thank the person for reading your letter, and ask for a reply. Give your name and address, and perhaps your age. Consider sending a similar letter to your local newspaper. And don't forget to have your friends and others write too!

Planet Care = Peace

One of the most recent winners of the Nobel Peace Prize is Professor Wangari Maathai. She is a Kenyan woman who started the Green Belt Movement in 1977. This movement encourages women, children, and all citizens to plant trees and care for the environment.

INTERNET RESOURCES

Attention Planet Patrolers, the libraries are filled with great field guides to insects, birds, mammals, trees, and even rocks! Libraries also carry books and movies on all the great topics in this book, and every exciting animal and plant in the world. So explore!

The Internet is another great source of information. Below are some sites that offer current information and interactive activities.

GENERAL

http://www.usda.gov/news/usdakids/index.html Kids' pages on many topics, including the earth, nature, and health.

www.epa.gov/kids/ Kids' page for the U.S. Environmental Protection Agency has information on species, global warming, garbage, recycling, and other environmental subjects.

WILDLIFE WATCH

http://educators.fws.gov/S_contacts.html The U.S. Fish & Wildlife Service's listing of great links for students researching wildlife and habitats. Links include pages on the department's own website as well as other reputable sites

http://mbgnet.mobot.org Site by Missouri Botanical Gardens with information on the world's biomes, freshwater and marine ecosystems, shorelines, and tropical and temperate oceans

http://endangered.fws.gov/kids/ The U. S. Fish & Wildlife Service's Kids' Corner

www.kidsplanet.org/factsheets/esa.html Defenders of Wildlife fact sheet on endangered species

http://www.nrcs.usda.gov/feature/backyard/ Backyard Habitat Information from the USDA

www.nwf.org/backyardwildlifehabitat/ National Wildlife Federation's Backyard Habitat Program

www.wildeducation.org/programs/hab_2000/hab2000.asp Canadian habitat program

www.nwf.org/schoolyardhabitats/ National Wildlife Federation's Schoolyard program

www.earthspan.org/Education.htm Eye of the Falcon wildlife education program

www.nrcs.usda.gov/feature/education/squirm/skworm.html USDA information for kids on soil conservation

http://school.discovery.com/schooladventures/soil/index.html "The Dirt on Soil" (grades 5-8) from Discovery School

http://www.enature.com/audio/audio_home.asp Samples of birdsongs from eNature

http://www.audubon.org/educate/expert/ Links to great information sites on birds

http://www.bear-tracker.com/index.html Animal tracking information

http://www.learner.org/jnorth/orientation/About.html Join a global study of wildlife migration and seasonal change

www.iwla.org/sos Izaak Walton League's Save Our Stream Program

http://www.epa.gov/owow/nps/nps_edu/index.html EPA information for kids on water pollution

http://www.mbayaq.org/lc/ Monterey Bay Aquarium kids' pages

ECO-CHALLENGES

www.smogcity.com/welcome.htm A game-like site showing how choices add up to smog

www.epa.gov/airnow/aqikids/index.html EPA's color-coded air quality index

http://www.pewclimate.org/global-warming-basics/kidspage.cfm Information on global warming and climate changes

http://www.rainforest-alliance.org/resources/forest-facts/index.html Information on rain forests and how to protect them

www.treemusketeers.org Kids' organization for tree planting

www.arborday.org/kids/kidsdif.cfm Kids making a difference by tree planting

http://www.amsa.gov.au/Marine_Environment_Protection/Educational_resorces_and_information/Kids/Fix_a_slick.asp The Fix-a-Slick Game

DAILY DEFENSE

http://www.epa.gov/recyclecity/ EPA's kids' recycling pages
http://flint.apogee.net/kids/default.aspx Kids' pages on energy history, sources, and alternatives
www.nrel.gov/education/students/natjiss.html Junior Solar Sprint
http://www.globalschoolnet.org/GSH/project/gg/ GeoGame through the collaborative global learning site. The home site has many other interesting activities.
http://www.peacecorps.gov/kids/ Explore the world with this game
http://www.un.org/Pubs/CyberSchoolBus/index.asp United Nations' student pages and games
www.kidsplanet.org Kids' page for the Defenders of Wildlife organization
www.kidsforsavingearth.org Kids for Saving the Earth organization

KEY WORDS

acid rain: rain that has mixed with chemicals from air pollution. The polluted rain can harm plants and add dangerous chemicals to lakes, rivers, ponds, and wetlands.

biodegradable: able to rot, or break down, into natural, harmless substances

biodiesel fuels: automobile fuels made from plant oils such as soybean oil. They are called renewable fuels, because we can always grow more plants to make more fuel.

clear cutting: cutting down all the trees in an area at one time

compost: a mixture of plant material that is left to rot until it turns into a rich fertilizer for gardens and farm fields

diversity: the presence of a variety of species in one habitat

ecologist: a person who studies how living things relate to each other and their environment

endangered: at risk of dying out and becoming extinct

erode: to wear away the soil. Erosion is caused by wind or moving water.

exotic species: species that have been introduced to an environment where they do not normally live

extinct: no longer alive anywhere on earth. The dodo is an extinct species of bird.

global warming: the slow warming of the earth caused by too much carbon dioxide in the air

habitat: the place in nature where a plant or animal makes its home

interdependency: the many relationships between different species that allow them all to survive together

invasive species: species that have been introduced to a new environment and cause problems for the species already living there

microorganism: a living thing so small that it is only visible under a microscope

migratory: living part of the year in one location and the rest of the year in one or more distant locations

native species: species that naturally live in a certain place

nutrients: substances that provide nutrition

ozone layer: a layer of gases that surrounds the earth and protects the planet from the sun's harmful rays

pollution: substances or objects that change the natural state of air, water, or habitats. Trash, loud noise, smoke, and chemicals are some things that cause pollution.

population: the total number of a certain species in an area

predator: an animal that kills other animals for food

recycle: to turn used items into new materials or products

renewable energies: power sources that do not run out, such as sunlight and wind power

sediment: bits of soil, plant matter, and chemicals that settle to the bottom in a liquid

selective cutting: a method in which some trees in an area are cut down for lumber while other trees are left in place

solar powered: driven by energy collected from sunlight

species: one particular kind of living thing. Humans are a species, and so are black-capped chickadees.

sustainable: using a resource (such as forests or farmland) in careful ways to keep it from being used up or permanently damaged

threatened: at risk of becoming endangered

topsoil: the surface layer of soil, which is richest in the nutrients plants need

wilderness: areas of land left wild, motorless, and not permanently changed by humans

INDEX